i can't go back to sleep

selected poems

EMMANUEL JOHNSON

I Can't Go Back to Sleep: Selected Poems

First published in 2024.

Cover design: Godswill Ezeonyeka

ISBN: 9798872542780

For everyone with words they never could express.

Contents

V

I Am Held in Space Afloat

Interlude V *by* Godswill Ezeonyeka

One Thing Truly Never Left

Walking Again

The Wilderness Trek

Eternity in My Heart

The Secret Place

Closing Nights

Blessed Assurance

At Midnight

Finding Joy

Downtrodden

The Path of the Just

Do Not Destroy

Eternal New Day

Words I Never Could Express I

Words I Never Could Express II

Peace, Yet Again

Midnight Thoughts

When the Lights Fade

When My Time Comes

Visions of Home II

Preface

Hey there, welcome. You know, it has taken me a while to think of how best to open this book. I thought, maybe have a dialogue between two fictional characters, or an abstract piece on a philosophical subject, or simply proceed directly to the poems. But I decided to write instead, to express my thoughts simply and 'come clean.' My purpose for writing this preface is to provide an idea of why I made this book, and additional information you should know about its content.

I started writing poems in 2018 to deal with pressing thoughts and feelings, to express and make sense of them. Since then, I have found poetry to be a really useful outlet of self-expression for me. Through it, I have expressed difficult feelings, thoughts and observations I have noted in life experiences. In the process of making this book, I have recognised the significance of documenting the aforementioned points. Because every moment that is lived is infinitely significant, in that, there is a complex world of meaning by which we are surrounded. This world of meaning presents opportunities for reflection. In these

9

moments of reflection, I have written poems which reflect my interaction with our shared meaningful world. The poems in this book present a representation of my world, and it was my desire to make this book to capture this representation in one piece.

In addition to my poems, there are 5 poems written by my friends: Maybelle, Adetiloye, George Akomas jr and Godswill Ezeonyeka, which I use as interludes in the book. All interludes are preceded with an image photographed by the writer of the subsequent interlude. I use these interludes to steer the course of the book's story as it transitions between 5 chapters to deliver a message. The message it delivers is this: you are welcome here and invited to share in my experience. I encourage you to read my poems with a desire to take something personal from it for yourself.

Emmanuel Johnson

I

That Moment

Contemplations I

As I share my stories with you,
from this trip I embarked,
I acknowledge I have come to realise
a thing called reality,
which often catches up on you,
no matter how far ahead you seem to be.

Interlude I *by* Maybelle

Despair...
searching for its snaking roots;
Is it the thought that you'll never be enough.
The feeling of being adrift upon a vast sea
The likelihood that you alone are left behind.
Or the fear of unsatisfactory pursuit.
Despair...
Hands clutching heart
Tears drenched cheeks
Icy fingers of fear snaking through.
Despair...
It falls like a dark cloud upon a sunny day
An eclipse falling suddenly
The earth shaking and your feet lost
Numb, deaf and unseeing.
Despair...
it happens.

The Deep End

I feel like I'm bubbling,
revolving, moving in angles and
showing sides.
I feel like I'm struggling,
I'm toughening up,
but I'm showing signs,
of one who is concentrated,
elevated, to the top of outburst,
but well devoted,
to the path before me,
getting it, and getting it right is a must.
In drawbacks of recollection,
my hands are held, high up, and my eyes down,
low in through the weekend,
the verses of the version,
stuffed, punched and hidden way down
through the deep end.

Aloneness

I can't hear my voice.
This is the best location to send my message.
I got comfortable,
I realised this a while ago but I wasn't concerned.
What's changed now is,
nothing makes sense anymo--
nothing makes sense anymore.
There is a constant recording
which plays over.
Inaudible but present,
when he goes to sleep
when he wakes up
when he exists.
My voice eloped in corner space,
and so did i.

Face to Face

Thoughts skimming through my mind,
jumping high as grasshoppers,
swift and difficult to get hold of.
My place on the ground is in contention
as I face the challenge of clarity.
What is my place and where do I belong?
My answers are blur and abstract.
I make a deliberate attempt to be clear.
I rest in the warm embrace of the strings
as the deliberation looks to extend until morning.

Pandemonium

Looking on,
seated in the square of things that move,
all the while still.
Trying to connect to that which will fulfil.
Other things blur out at this point,
the mind stretches out at this point.
The soul attempts to speak but is lost in translation;
desires jump in, in a quest for attention;
the heart enveloping as always
that which it sees.
All the while, the focus is narrow;
the focus is clear:
the never ending crave to step out and belong.

Speechless

As the space here reverberates,
I sit in a kind of stillness.
Not one thought of as tranquil,
but one which cries out,
saying 'let it out let it out let it out!'
Let what out?

Restless

Here now, there soon.
Tumbling, up, down,
dizzy oblivion soon.
Good break now,
a nice break from the chaos.
Rumbling here now,
an interlude short lived.

In motion, get there.
Drifting, left, right,
take me there.
The cool place,
an encounter of stroll and breeze.
Falling in place,
a harvest well suited.

Tired

Nothing seems to satisfy.
I am too short of words to
extend this with more context.

Visions of Home I

Feelings not expressed
Feelings too difficult to be expressed.
Moments felt and lived
Moments too distant to be felt and lived.
People seen and touched
People too far to be seen and touched.
Memories held and felt
Memories too distant to be held and felt.
Images seen and lived
Images too distant to be seen and lived.
Sounds heard and felt
Sounds too distant to be heard and felt.

Time, the constant observer
Time too near, waiting on my response.

Life-Pump I

I am weak,
but I trust you still.
It feels like I might stumble,
but I trust you still.
Smokes of doubt are infiltrating,
but I trust you still.
I'm at my breaking point,
but I trust you still.
The corners of my mind panic and shift,
but I trust you still.
You are the light of my life,
you are the light of my life,
you are the light of my life.
You are the flag bearer of my saving race.

It's There

Revive my soul, I say,
as the shadows of regret
bring no satisfaction to me.
The rolling of the pines
which ignited, a memory away,
makes sense no longer,
as the frontier of my direction
now heads towards loftier heights.
Revive my soul again, I say,
though my steps miss or land.
Though whatever outcome,
the glimpse of your face
makes way for a yearning
of eternal companionship,
far away from the not so distant
ever approaching threshold of uncertainty.

Locked onto You

Spreading out,
starting all over.
In the face of this enormous gulf,
making plain the demarcation
between foot and ground.
The fall is deep and piercing,
as left and right are called upon
to intervene, but to no response.
Through the panic,
the lowly dove swivels,
crying out to what is left
of the stagnated heart;
I welcome you,
I bless you.
You are safe in my warm embrace.

Haven of Newness

In the haven of newness
I see, my source of hope.
This newness; it's His; now mine.
My newness.
I am safe in this newness.
His newness; my newness.
Nothing matters in this newness.
Everything is alright in this newness.
I am sheltered; I am reborn.
I am overwhelmed.
I feel, but differently.
I live, I die, in this newness.

Confidence

Bestowed upon me
in my hand to hold;
the gracious giver has blessed my soul.
The calming sounds passing on
when I close my eyes,
provide comfort, peace and assurance,
which guide my path.

My Saving Grace

The mark shall always point
to the breaking dawn,
which outpaced my sorrows
and set my life right,
giving me something to live for everyday.
I set aside all appearances of darkness,
and put on the armour of light,
in honour of whom I owe it all to,
my saving grace.

Comforter

Some day,
I shall learn of words that describe you:
a painting of things within.
Things within.
Things within me,
which cannot be expressed.
Until that day,
one day, some day,
I shall feel your warm embrace.
As you sit beside me,
loudly, whispering, silent,
words, which cannot be expressed.

II

When Words Come Alive

Interlude II *by* Adetiloye

I want to write,
I have to write,
I can't go back to sleep,
Bewildered by moonlight,
Stuck in the blues,
Blueing not of a broken heart,
But brewing this life of art.

I can't go back to sleep,
Maybe I should write,
Maybe I have to write,
When it comes down to it,
It's what I have left,
This pen, these words,
This heart, this art,
If anything is taken away,
Even my sleep;
Dreams of a vision to spur,
I'll have to write.

Do Not Be in a Hurry to Grow Up I

First and foremost
I want you to see what I see.

The dead-looking branches wiggle in my direction,
a personal testimony shared intimately
between us two, and the congregation of the lifeworld.
They wiggle, as to say
'be reminded of my essence,
do not stray from my essence.
Your walk from place to place
speaks to my shared message.'
I sit upright and revere in my limits.
I can't go back to sleep.

The Nature of Days

These days,
I see things take a turn here
and another there.
The straight path which once was
creates ever-forming interlinks
I now try to make sense of.
I am conflicted.
My observation of its nature keeps me
perplexed, as I see same and others
hide beneath the same mask.
In the final analysis,
I realise a dedication
to get to the root of this,
and prevailing situations
which obstruct my search,
as I continually seek meaning.

Shifting Shadows

Perhaps the most constant literary struggle I have faced is this: not having sufficient words to express what I see going on before me. As a result, I am brought unceasingly to the same starting point, of attempting to make sense of what I see going on before me.

On Feelings

Perhaps I ought to not write about feelings,
perhaps I ought to 'get out of my feelings,'
whatever that means.

Perhaps I ought to critique feelings,
perhaps I ought to drown myself in feelings.
Perhaps I ought to express my feelings unashamedly.

Whatever the case may be,
I am not concerned at this moment
about outside conceptions of my life.
So I say as I wrestle persistently with that lie.

On Desire

I wonder what it is about desire
that swivels within layers of layers.
I unfold and unfold but I find more layers.
I contemplate upon these layers
but I find unfolding questions.
Were I to put into words what I see,
I would remain stuck in a standstill.
Yet desire ravages on the inside,
yearning to be expressed.
I lay me down in silence
and stillness of thought.
I hold onto what I do not see.
I say to myself,
'I will wait for you.'

On Coincidence

Why did this happen?
This happens, that happened.
I don't understand why that happened.
I would be fooling myself,
speaking out of utter arrogance
if I claimed to understand why it did.
If my choice was mildly out of place,
I would be in a different place now.
A different place may produce a different outcome,
a different outcome may produce a different life.
What if I made a different choice?
In my pursuit of truth, I stumble upon
a realisation of human finitude.
I don't get to make all choices
so I don't get to see all things.
I don't get to see all things
so I don't get to know all things.
I feel humbled as I return where I started.
I won't ask why it happened,
I'll simply acknowledge that it did.

On Choice

Choice,
what's right to do.
What to do?
Uncertain, that to do.
What to do?
Make a choice.
Eyes open, supposedly.
What's right to do.
Uncertain, what's right to do.
Make a choice!

Ways of the Mind

Moving in not so distant space
though seated still,
the mind flounders;
its grip steeps deep and grips on.
To ends unknown, its move extends;
in paths unclear, its wander unfolds.
Its state undermined,
as it makes its move;
closer and closer
to the centre of devotion,
which pleads, on bent knees,
for the acknowledgment of truth:
the closing of the ceremony.

Sailing On

Navigating,
steering left, right.
Moving, on the move;
tropical entities of familiar memory behind,
distant coverings of newness ahead.
Memory memory,
thoughtful musings from the present standpoint,
as I look on the ancient building.
Precious monumental heritage I now stand on,
however distant it may be.

Unceasing Jewel

The runway of chance,
it meanders deep and deep,
its variety, clear to see,
I wish it allotted fairly to all.

The highway uncertain,
mysterious in view,
all wretched, the passersby,
all planed unevenly.

The runway of time,
its beauty, unimaginable,
its splendour, blinding,
all cascades of ignored value.

A Subject Among Subjects

Why do you look on me with such contempt?
You start off on one point,
then gain access to another.
I am the subject of your infiltrating gaze,
as you ramp up;
skimming on and beyond,
mid and low,
now and then.
My intricacies are exposed.
Time is zooming out on me.

Fight the Good Fight

Half awake, half asleep.
My hands are spread wide,
my back is one with the ground.
In light of this moment,
I see time clearly,
in all its glory; masked and unmasked,
as he takes an extended walk of grandeur.
I take this moment into the palm of my hand,
I take grip of his very colourful cloak.
As he turns around to behold the gasper,
he is drawn to share in his very significant situation.
In response to this occurrence,
he bends and whispers:
'this is it,
this is it.'

Hourglass

Surrounded by the coast,
the main character maintains in scepticism,
while laying on moisturised sand.
His thoughts creep and cripple,
hint and hinder,
peek and pierce.
Far to fathom,
farther away than desired,
he stretches out anyway,
in hopeful expectation,
to grab onto the certain.
Trapped in the painted cage,
his efforts prove pointless.
Time to re-strategise,
time to unlearn,
unlearn to relearn,
relearn to re-know,
re-know what he knew.
He knew all along,
how did he get here?

Characters in the Big Tale

The sunshine,
it flashes through mere thoughts,
mere thoughts of what you are like,
or what you could be like?
The coming days look back with
a firm conviction in the eye.
A depthless world unveils in those eyes,
as a gaze is transmitted back and forth.
Though ushered in with feelings
of unease about uncertainties,
the character delights in
extravagances of you and I.

Vignette in Passing

The moment that was felt
in the vignette in close,
which kept ablaze the light that shines
for delights to be seen as delights.
Shaped in close, in spaces once lived and shaped by
distant others,
now leased to thine for new shaping,
which shall last only for a moment.
This opportunity shall not be missed,
but maximised in the fast-paced time afforded.
The break in the moment amongst moments is truly
unforgettable,
as the farfetched was held for keeps.
The holder is left grateful for the vignette,
as he lives to see, the sickness in the self
taken away for dazzling splinters of the time.

Disillusioned

This glass, though once whole,
now lies shattered, in drifting pieces.
Its turnaround spots reveal a hurt,
a hurt which so earnestly masks
intricacies of its one true vulnerability.
One true vulnerability is replicated,
now, in drifting pieces,
a failed attempt it is,
at concealing its intricacies.
Nevertheless, in its farewell sweep,
it is looked back
as a hardened labourer,
immune of all vulnerability.
What a sad and untrue end
to an experience this is,
the writer remarks.

Do Not Be in a Hurry to Grow Up II

The observer maintains in humble thought.
The branches sprout forth new life to the observer's
surprise.
Tertiary connectors make themselves known in the
vicinity.
This is the situation of the moment.

In majestic new apparel
the branches radiate a sense of grace.
One which appears to come from long negotiations
with time.
There may be meaning to this.
The observer takes note and retreats to solitude.

The experience of solitude is an opportunity for deep
thought.
Meanings become personal.
I contemplate on what I just experienced.
I don't know what I just experienced.
I recount in final analysis on what is right.
I devote to walk the rest of my days
in ways of meaningful observation.

III

The Final Laps Repeat

Interlude III *by* Maybelle

In this big small world
Under the vastness of the skies
I am but a speck, a blot if you will
Living in retrospect
The road not taken
The steps not taken
Am I simply unseeing
Or do I lack understanding.
I wonder; what would life have
been on the other side?
The many roads not taken
And the many wrong turns made.

Memories

Memories screech in circles,
Memories lived, memories not lived.
For memories not lived
I see a beauty of what could be,
I behold a promise not made.
Memories lived and felt remain
deep in the heart with outpourings of affection.
These affections offer a promise not made
of memories not lived.
As the downpour ensues
I hold onto both memories.
As the billows intensify
I hold on tightly with all my strength.

Euphoric

Venturing, through the corridors
of thrill and bliss, in this:
a joy to light my face, and yours,
for tomorrow, we dismiss.
Too far to go through the village,
but close, to the swan on lane.
Past flashing dreams across the stage,
and hope to the last of pain.
Indeed, those days were true,
a joy to light my face, and yours.
I still think about you,
venturing, through the corridors.

Reminisces of the Bright Blue Sky

This little thing going on here
has become the centre of my focus,
at least for a moment or more;
unlike anything experienced before.
Under the comfort of the generous shed,
I lay in awe, unshackled,
as I made it my duty to assemble
the army of bloom in my mental sky
into a cohesive unit;
testifying of the uniqueness of an experience.
As the occasion drew to a close,
I remained asleep
and missed the goodbye ceremony.
This note details the highlight
of the hopeful expedition.
You are my shining star.

Pick Yourself Up

I recount that my sky
looked brighter a minute ago.
Little appearances of light
passing on nearby surfaces
extend a hand of warmth.
The breeze conducts the lifeworld
to motions of such gentle harmony.
I hold on to watch this rendition.
I stay on till embrace of dawn.
I let go of your hold on me.
I am visited at my point of need.

Seasons

In days past,
we walked together, we shared everything;
what we had, what we did not.
The strands of time co-shared then,
the strands of time partake now.
Though our walk splits into multiple ends,
we co-partake now in a shared experience:
a dream we dreamed,
of a day to come;
when our walk prospers,
when our expectations draw close,
and our tribulations end.
And on the anticipated day,
our flowers hit the soil of becoming,
and we know that surely, we shall walk together again.

My Evening Muse

My muse for the evening,
I delight at the sight of you.
Time looks on, on gatekeeping duties,
I hold on, to the last second in passing.
Enjoined, hand to hand,
in the embrace of the breeze.
I rejoice in contentment
of yesterday's striving.
It led me to you,
and for that I'm thankful.
My muse for the evening,
tonight's walk has reached its close.
I do not sorrow over what was not,
I rejoice in hope
of tomorrow's glory.
Until then,
we wait.
Hands joined,
under the sky
of hope,
we wait.
Eyes fixed,
over the certainty
of things hoped for,
we wait.

We are Moving

I feel like,
I feel like I am contemplating but I don't know what I
am thinking about.
There is a hovering,
it feels like silence but sounds like a certain wavering
attuned.
What would tomorrow be like?

I Need You

Are you here?
Please?
I'm awake and trying to reach you,
somehow.
Anyhow possible.
Please respond, I miss your touch.

Devotion

I'm shivering,
I don't feel great,
I don't feel great at all.
I've been shut out,
while the celebrations go on inside.
My hands hurt from knocking,
I wish to be welcomed again inside,
but come what may,
if it happens or it doesn't,
here is where you'll find me,
speaking life until it comes alive.

Lived Pieces

The trek at work,
which circled in motion,
though stagnant in the primary spot.
That trek, who knew,
would go, just to return, unceasingly.
Though ceasing, at least, as it seems,
when its brightness is not seen, it deems,
as the moving path presents itself in the present.
As soon noticed, it remains,
even as the colourful panics kick in.

Living Space

My living space is my best friend.
My living space is my most intimate enemy.
I can't break out of expectations of
who I'm meant to be.
Expectations of what having a PhD
is meant to represent.
I am phased in my living space,
face to face with me.
I am fazed in my living space,
face to face with who I am meant to be.
Face to face with what I am meant to be doing.
Facing, this phase.
I don't feel like I can get past this phase.

Joys of Sobriety

Basking in this humble moment,
it feels as though the ulterior
bears little significance.
This is strongly evident,
particularly with the companionship
of the crying sound on mute,
which infiltrates into the innermost
chambers of the heart.
What a blissful experience this is,
though other passions now moan,
while on the lengthy queue,
on the aisle that knows no end,
as they too expect a turn,
before the closing of
tonight's entertainment.

States of Isolation

Acquainted with you again;
truly, you are no new companion
because I have shared moments of
reason, laughter and sadness with you for many,
many years.
But now, called into question by this new state,
I ask myself more truthfully:
can I recognise you any longer?
You seem very different this time around.
The state I find myself misleads;
I work reasonably to find a way around it.
But as I get to witness more states around,
I realise ever static banalities
which shaped past encounters and meanings.
Now I find that very interesting.

Making Sense of a Filmmaker's Block I
Experienced While in Social Isolation

This time, I am unsettled.
In the feelings department.
I make use of my mind.
It is what I know best.
It is my favourite deviation.
I soak whole bodied in water.
I am unable to feel.

Midnight Phases

There is a thought I find comforting,
worth cherishing,
worth holding onto.

That, this which I can point to,
which I feel
which I hold,
is of greater purpose.

I am empty without this contribution,
this value from my experience,
which you find comforting,
worth cherishing,
worth holding onto.

Legacy

I'm too weak to type
but too drawn to ignore.
I have a thing
on the inside
that cries out,
night and day,
wishing to be
expressed.
I don't think
it can be
expressed
sufficiently,
because
words
fail,
as we know.
But maybe,
the point isn't
to say it fully,
maybe it is
to leave a mark,
so others may taste,
and see, the glory of the Lord.

It is Well

Crying out to the horizons;
so often I have felt the voice radiate in waves.
Impacting, bouncing and hitting flexible lines,
only to rub off and remain on sitting ground.
Its focus right here and now is clear:
to attain the unamendable,
as it tiptoes past the days ahead.
Joy shall be optimum
when the voice returns,
with arms wide open,
crying out through the eternities,
I take you in and bless you;
you are welcome here.

Life-Pump II

There seems to be a feeling of displacement
out and about.
This is my feedback,
my personal statement,
pencilled across the surface of light,
where heat radiates to alleviate of sorrow.

My ordeal once again is to make sense
of this phase.
In thoughts and writings
which are clear to understand.
Past moments of clarity and colour,
are now to be understood,
as I sleep and wake to contemplation.

I conclude that the clarity and colour I felt
were surely real.
There is no good thing without you.
I sit, lay, walk, talk, all in emptiness.
In stillness, I feel restless still.
Darkness is my closest friend, without you.
When the curtains are drawn at night,
I find that you are the light of my life, still.

Life-Pump III

The end of a matter
is greater than its start.
So I look up,
in discouragement.
I look up, in pain,
I look up, in sorrow.
I make my petitions
and I make them plain.
Just because I don't see you
doesn't mean you never came.

The Blinkering Connection

I am in an in-between space.
My right hand is stretched out,
I am trying to connect with you.
In this space, I feel a cold hovering,
which wallows around the surface of my skin,
only to make a stagnant abode on the same
surface it explores.
But, my desire is unchanged,
I am trying to connect with you.
I sense a kind of uncertain reception,
I am unable to dive in any further.
Upon the halt of my outstretched right hand,
I let out the best of my heart's virtue.
Though inaudible in voice,
this is what it says in essence:
'I am weak, you are strong,
I want some of that radiant love in my life,'
as I am still trying to connect with you today.

Intermission

Judge me Lord.
You see my heart.
You see the hidden words I am unable to express.

IV

I Turn Away for a Moment

Interlude IV

by George Akomas jr

I can't go back to sleep
For fear lies on the other side
The terrors I buried came alive
Will keep them at bay with my waking mind.

I can't go back to sleep
For the dawn is already here
And you have kept me up all night
Whispering over the phone sweetly into my ear.

I can't go back to sleep
Cos I dreamt that you were
still alive
And that life was my nightmare
but now awake
Can't bear to go through it again, I just won't survive.

I can't go back to sleep
You look so beautiful sleeping next to me
Fears I will fail you or you hurt me are gone
Wish I could freeze now for eternity.

I can't go back to sleep
Tasted of the fruits of the living tree
More alive than woke, you have shown me
How beautiful my life awake can be.

Auto

Auto walking.
Layers concealed, hidden within.
A walk embarked,
control lost in-between.
Auto running.
Stomps to ground, impact unfelt.
The chest tightens,
climactic finale, panting ensues.
Auto flying.
Back on cushion, breath set loose.
A moment of rest,
grips let loose, sensitivity heightens.

The Running Man

He knows no bend,
he knows no bend.
The running man lives on,
drinking from the cup of uncertainty.
That said out loud
in clear terms,
as his finish line is ever prolonged.
He knows no bend,
he knows no bend,
but this he knows,
with all his heart,
with all his soul,
with all his strength:
in his lonely, obscure tunnel covered in darkness,
the only light radiates from the cross.

Wandering Heart

O wandering heart of mine,
I trace your tracks up this hill
but I do not see where you go.
Day and night you wander,
paying little heed to burnout.
Across all entrances and exits
you dash simultaneously,
drifting unreservedly.
I trace your movements
but only find traces
of questions you leave behind.
I cannot understand your tracks,
they are unimaginably complex.
I cannot number your steers,
they are infinite in number.
You disperse in prideful splendour
to flounder in collective shatter.
Your pride-filled ways mislead,
moving but going nowhere precise.
Your words are multi-minded,
yet you push to enforce your will.
You wail with outbursts of desire,
yet, enroute your solo dash,
you desire nothing ultimately meaningful.

Camp Fire

Wide spaced,
running in-between,
I move from space to space,
exploring what outside offers.
Left, right, hands swinging low,
as I make my strides, brushing past the grass.
I am yet to arrive at my destination,
but it will be worth the journey.

Spectacles

I made my colour a home,
to be sheltered, nurtured
and protected from images.

Images move in sublime,
threatening to shatter my backbone.
I feel inanimate, imagined untruthfully.

To protect my sanity,
I made my colour a home,
it lights my mental sky,
it keeps a smile on my face.

It's Not All about You

'This straight path now chosen
shall mark the start of the new,'
so he says.
'The crooked shall be straight,
never to be readjusted,'
so he says.
'The body and tongue shall,
and must, walk in unison,'
so he says.

The fixed will resumes its bend,
as the heart spills,
yes it does.
The crouching pleasure ignites
titillating rubs,
yes it does.
The old, parades in a shiny cloak
of renewed appeal,
yes it does.

Don't grieve the one you love.

Moment of Truth

The beginning comes.
It goes on and on.
Excitement comes, goes.
Here, not here.
Fleet the thrills; empty days.
Empty days, catching up.
Catching up to me
but not caught me.
One thing, maintaining:
the light that came and stayed.
The light; the truth, the life:
the light who comes, on and on.
On and on, the beginning comes,
but the beginning will never be the end.

There Came a Time

Searching for something;
unaware I was and what it was.
Watching days pass like shifting shadows;
viewing time in front, side, and back.
Looking vaguely for long,
being misled by false acuity.
The links disconnected and then I saw,
my severed paradigm.
Would you talk to me, my dear paradigm?
How I need you now, my dear paradigm.
Your love stayed strong, even when I faltered.
And now I see,
that secret understanding between us,
which you tried to make me see earlier.
O how illusioned I was,
my redemptive paradigm.

Heart-Cry

Redeem me,
I cry out to you, my God.
Save me from the wretched grasp of dust.
I call on you,
you never fail me.
When others judge and misunderstand me,
you show grace and mercy to me.
Comfort me
and embrace me in your unfailing love.
In your presence
I find peace, amidst all shadows of sorrow.
Touch me and make me whole,
I pray.

You

Purify me Lord,
make me clean.
I hunger all day,
in ways unclear.
My heart speaks,
I don't know
its echoes,
it's a blur to me.
But I sense in some way,
something deeper than words.
In ways simple in mystery,
I know, though on my knees,
your dream for me is actually real.
Lead me to it, Lord,
my heart yearns for oneness.

Passing Days

Heart shatter,
pieces drift near and far.
The scene is set in light some days,
days drifting in blips of light.
With few words in my heart,
I lay in warmth with eyes shut,
watching, waiting,
waiting for your touch,
yearning for your embrace.

Contemplations II

Lord,
I desire something substantial
but can't express adequately
in words, the feelings I have
that describe it.

Moving with a Spirit of Contentment

Engaged in this occasion;
right here, where I happen to find myself
is truly special.
Very ordinary and special.
Humility and contentment guiding,
bright doors opening all around.
Peaceful winds blowing through the interstices,
made possible by the chaos.
The sounds of love envelope my heart,
as I sit by and look through the window of hope.
The heart remains calm,
the mighty waters rush in.
I am endowed with all I need.

Essential to Now

Stillness in motion,
hands firm, legs interlocked,
practising the devotion
of staying calm and soaking in.
The cool is warm,
at finger-tipping touch.
The light drills its way in,
my soul is revived again.

Beauty Splinters

Empty.
I feel empty.
I surf on slides of uncertainty,
I make my way breathlessly.
I need you, desperately.
I need you more than life.
In need you are my life.
I need you, desperately.

Hope.
Fill me up.
I need you, desperately.
With you I rest in confidence.
In the depths, you heal like none else.
In the morning, I wake to assuredness.
In you, I find my confidence.
I need you, desperately.

Peace.
Be with me.
Though days sing songs uncertain,
though nights look deep in void,
you clothe me in beauty splinters,
you lift my head, I look to you.
In you, you are my confidence.
I need you, desperately.

Looking Up with a Kind of Fervent

Reverence

As I am drawn to you today,
I look up in utmost sincerity,
with a shaky heart
stirring in noble reception,
to your heavy downpour of love,
and grace; my everything.
Your tender love,
though not always embraced,
remains unchanging,
despite the pandemonium
between hands of self and grip.
But even though
I see otherwise sometimes,
your life, your love,
your peace, your grace,
are all I need,
as I am drawn to you today.

Night Sky

Is it okay if I have nothing
to give of myself today?
Though, for this day
I have looked on
in anticipation
and wonder.

I wonder, sometimes,
if I appreciated yesterday enough,
or spent it elsewhere,
in thoughts of where I might be today.

Though I felt the need to immerse in today,
I caved in to fear and surrendered
at the tease of my imagination.

But, today is the day,
not yesterday or tomorrow.
The high lines are before me now,
to touch, see and feel. I shall waste time no longer.

The Word

I look to you.
I look to you.
I look to you.

My words rise and fall,
pressured by weights too heavy.

When words fail
I look to you.
Let your word carry what I can't.

Your word pierces soul and spirit,
judging thoughts of the heart.
My words rise and fall.
Let your word carry what I can't.

Your word is alive and active,
turning darkness to light.
Your word is alive and active,
creating things not yet seen.

Refiner's Fire

Here I am
on my walk through the everyday.
Searching for you, but finding you instead.
Hovering over, pricking deeper.
I light my feet,
I am embraced by truth.
Now I see,
the blueprint for the days.
The days, your days; now my days.
That thorn, in my flesh
now oil, for my head.
Now I see,
on my walk through the everyday,
I am not alone, I never was.

Open Hearted

In the midst of chaos,
I open myself up.
Surrounded, literally and figuratively,
by dangers out to wield and possess.
In the midst of this chaos,
I open myself up.
Vulnerable, in the most basic form of intent,
dangers paying no heed to my vulnerability.
In the belly of this chaos,
I open myself up.
Comforted, attended to by perfect love,
coming to my rescue to cast out all fear.

Salvation

In the midst of the desolate paths,
where that which does not move flies,
and one who does not talk screams;
therein, therein, the light of all time beams;
the contrite surrenders in his glory,
and is embraced in the warmth of his love.

Thank You for Saving Me

High in the deepest of pits,
my face exudes contentment.
With you in my inmost focus,
I find a silent jubilant form.
The love you show to me
will be the beginning of me,
as I learn, locked in, steadfast
with the lowliest of hearts.
I feel the life of your words
echoed innermost existence.
It is important to be gracious to others.

No Looking Back

At the point of the shatter,
once distant glimmers blow up,
out of proportion.
In ways of absolute breathlessness,
the white flag is reintroduced in the scene
as the most ideal garment of choice.
Dizziness is certain,
as the antics of this merry-go-round
extend onto the lapse that is called final.
In the final analysis,
the simple truth is this:
I cried out, you saved me.
You are my everything.

V

I Am Held in Space Afloat

Interlude V

by Godswill Ezeonyeka

Divine predestination formed me in my sleep
Divine providence breathed the morning into me
Divine orchestration planted gardens but I slipped
Divine masterpiece exchanged my night for morning

I am the in-between of divine design
The drowsy wanderer in need of sleep and coffee
I am two worlds bound in drawn out divorce
To be or not to be, to sleep or not to sleep

I am mortal enemy to the man I want to be
A maleficent dragon fighting the prince of my being
I am valiant victor and vanquished villain
There is no way to win if I am at war with me

I am the in-between of divine disruption
A causeless curse caused my chaos to concede
I am startled sojourner and humbled human
A divine interruption has put to death my sleep.

One Thing Truly Never Left

This new journey of mine,
I have trodden; still treading.
Treading never ending.
Well, so it seems.
My days have been favoured coatings,
flavoured blisters in my mind,
ever pushing. Filters I now find,
ever reminding, like I ever forgot.
Well, maybe I did.
Filters crying out, every now and then,
never forget why you parted,
this is all you truly wanted.
To live the life in the count,
and walk the walk on the mount.
Living the life in the count,
walking the walk on the mount.

Walking Again

My feet are set in readiness for this,
my path is lit and eager to be trodden.
I am seated, as I observe
the cluster approaching within the shadows.
From a detailed glance, I notice his dried-up scars,
I see the grey fade in his eyes.
The path is set;
it is lit and eager to be trodden.
With this in mind, I make my move.
Now standing, I walk towards the cluster
with a kind of uncovering light,
which pierces through the hardest of surfaces.
Now faced, face to face with the cluster,
he says, in an unclear radiation:
'the fight has just begun,'
I say, in the covering of the light:
'goodness and mercy follow me all day.'

The Wilderness Trek

Becoming myself,
in majestic garments of time.
The fields once plain
had in it thorns through and through.
I contemplate on this:
the way one handles the banal,
as it walks with pride,
past the downcast face.
How I wish to lay hold of the certainty,
on that day, that the birds shall chirp for joy
and dry bones shall live again.

Eternity in My Heart

It is you and I again, fear.
We stand face to face
in confrontation,
as always.

Deep within, my soul trembles;
'what will become of me
if danger steps into
the sorrowful
garment of
actuality?'

What will be,
I do not know,
but this I attest to
with the core of my being:
I was born for a time such as this,
my functionality in the world matters,
my heart burdens in expansions of pain,
my heart rejoices because my anguish is gone.

The Secret Place

The light of life;
true cool for the troubled soul,
ever comforting, back then, right now.

Closing Nights

As long as you are with me,
I am happy
I am safe
I am complete.

Take me with you.
Wherever you go I go.
Wherever you dwell I dwell.
Whatever you hate I hate.
Whatever you are,
I shall be.

As the performers get ready to perform,
and the watchers get ready to watch;
in this grand hall filled with many colours,
right here shall I sit,
writing on the ground,
uttering words unlawful to be heard.

Blessed Assurance

I sing a song
in reverence of you.
I have a peace
that surpasses now,
I have a peace
that surpasses pain.

In life, I stand.
In death, I stand.
I stand in awe of you.
In uncertainty, I stand.
In convenience, I stand.
I sing in reverence of you.

At Midnight

My life is in the hand of the almighty.
I stand rest assured in the ultimate cool of certainty
which I now experience.
In view of the days ahead, I look on and wonder,
as I see many clouds in way of the actual way.
Shall it happen? I ask now and again,
as I remain, waiting, in the sojourning boat of time.
About these things, I know little;
but this I know
and stand rest assured;
that my life is in the hand of the almighty.

Finding Joy

Inflicted with deep restlessness;
I realise a desire for something eternal;
to put in plain words.
Words simply cannot:
they fail to express.
I try my best,
but I am unable to:
I fail to communicate.
But I know a knowing;
very true and trustworthy;
which never fails;
who always whispers:
there is that cosmic unity between us,
which nothing,
no one,
can take away.
No one can,
for I have beheld true joy.
My eyes have beheld true joy.

Downtrodden

The tide sees with it the fall,
which clamps and clashes,
washing away things of vibrant nature.
Severity is left deep in the pierce,
as the blessed surfer picks up from the piece.
The drop, the tear;
dripping never ending,
as the downtrodden surfer
puts in work for the final appearance.
From left to right,
the perfect mix of perfect picks,
as the victorious surfer rides on
the glorious assembled pieces.

The Path of the Just

Faithful and trustworthy saying,
resounded in me,
speeding past tunnels of time
to find me where I am.
Faithful and trustworthy saying,
ingrained in me,
with all majestic hope and expectation
from the ones who love me dearly,
with all their heart and might,
that one day, maybe
just maybe,
it shall turn out
to be my saving grace.
How faithful,
how trustworthy,
is the path of the shining light,
ever true,
that shines brighter and brighter,
unto the perfect day.
Abide by it, my child.

Do Not Destroy

I love you Lord.
You have delivered me from conflicts,
conflicts which threaten to harm my soul.
I say to my soul, 'the Lord is my hope and strength.'
You gird me securely in your perfect peace.
I sleep in anticipation of tomorrow because of you.
At night I said to myself,
'give me something, give me something.'
In the morning I now say,
'this is a beautiful day that you have made,
I will rejoice and be glad in it.'
All the days of my life are covered in your hand,
I am never alone because of your eternal love.

Eternal New Day

To turn my hurt to life.
I sit and contemplate.
Could it be, a reason for every hurt,
every mixed conflict,
moment of pain,
sorrow and disillusionment,
is eternal glory?
Eternal glory that outweighs hurt
and transforms to life?

I pause and contemplate.
I try to fix my eyes on what is eternal
but struggle.

Lord,
be a banner over me
and take me to the place you want me.
Like a leaf that falls and dillydallies mid-air,
I too dream to land on gentle waters,
that purify the soul
and unravel a renewed horizon
of hope unto a new day.

Words I Never Could Express I

Meeting in flashing points with you,
meetings lasting flashing moments.
I ponder in my heart,
how it would be to see you,
face to face.
To behold your immeasurable beauty,
the beauty which dashes across
in flashing moments.
I wish to lay hold of it.
By it, I am illuminated,
my life being the surface on which
this beauty shines.
Half asleep, I yearn for an awakening,
an awakening of my half-lit eyes by your beauty,
to see you face to face
and behold this beauty for myself.
I yearn for the day I shall see you face to face,
and behold this beauty for myself.

Words I Never Could Express II

I remind myself of you,
the morning bringing word of your mercies.
My life is in your hand,
this I say as I make my bed in you.

My soul desires something deeper,
the definition of which is you.
You are being itself,
the last point of reach.

Bring me to you,
I long for you constantly.
My words fail but yours resound,
in gentle echoes of my heart.

Peace, Yet Again

The hand of God is ever present, I see,
as I sit for a moment of reflection,
on where I am, how I got here,
and the trails of tomorrow
unfolding before me.

Your love,
my lifesaver,
shelters me tenderly,
in a world of chaos and darkness.

I lie in peace,
in reverence of something irreplaceable;
an eternal companionship.

Midnight Thoughts

The box falls and shatters,
glitters disperse to all corners.
The light in the midst of clusters shines,
despite the state of its surroundings.
I ponder on my bed,
I think of all the Lord has done.
The years spent on this chapter,
and the years to come.
The Lord looks on me in my surroundings,
He has mercy on my helpless estate.
The Lord whispers my name.
I say 'speak, for your servant is listening.'

When the Lights Fade

You are the best thing to happen to me.
The springs of my life shoot
with everlasting meaning
and encouragement for whatever
tomorrow shall bring.
Today, tomorrow,
now, forever,
happiness, sadness,
wisdom, folly,
are all meaningless without you.
My life was incomplete without you,
before you came by.
You complete my life, thank you for that.
I rejoice,
I bless the day,
I felt your touch.
The day I was reunited with your love.
The day I was reunited with your love.

When My Time Comes

The essence of being cries out,
some describe this cry as thought,
some as dream, others as feeling.
There is a cry that is not heard,
tears that pierce but are not seen,
groans that shake but are not felt.
The essence of being is crying out.
What is to be done with time?
What is to be done with finitude?
In time we are born,
in time we are gone.
In time we are young,
in time we are old.
In time we are simple,
in time we embrace wisdom.
What is to be done with time?
When my time comes
I wish to have made the best of my time.
When my time comes
I wish to have shared the best of me with others.
When that time comes
I wish to dwell in the place of rest,
to gaze upon His beauty and be comforted
by His splendour.

Visions of Home II

Images opening
Images opening
The essence of my being calls
The light of my essence adorns
Images opening
Images opening
My inner core has something to say
When shall I come and appear before God?

Printed in Great Britain
by Amazon